from SEA TO SHINING SEA

Kansas

By Dennis Brindell Fradin and Judith Bloom Fradin

CONSULTANTS

Homer E. Socolofsky, Ph.D., Emeritus Professor of History and University Historian,
Kansas State University

Robert L. Hillerich, Ph.D., Professor Emeritus, Bowling Green State University;
Consultant, Pinellas County Schools, Florida

CHILDRENS PRESS®

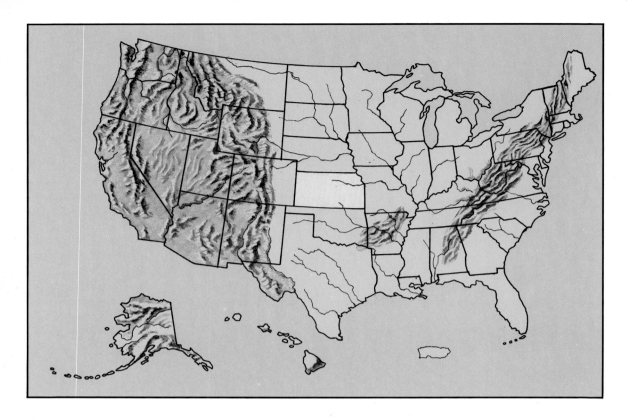

Kansas is one of the twelve states in the region called the Midwest. The other Midwest states are Illinois, Indiana, Iowa, Michigan, Minnesota, Missouri, Nebraska, North Dakota, Ohio, South Dakota, and Wisconsin.

For our cousins Bob, Larry, and Carol Wallace, with love

For his help, the authors thank Virgil W. Dean, historian and editor, Kansas State Historical Society

Front cover picture: An oil pumpjack in a wheat field near Hill City; page 1: Monument Rocks; back cover: Butterfly milkweed, Flint Hills Tallgrass Prairie, Butler County

Project Editor: Joan Downing
Design Director: Karen Kohn
Research Assistant: Michael Louis Fradin
Typesetting: Graphic Connections, Inc.
Engraving: Liberty Photoengraving

Library of Congress Cataloging-in-Publication Data

Fradin, Dennis B.
  Kansas / by Dennis Brindell Fradin & Judith Bloom Fradin.
    p.   cm. — (From sea to shining sea)
  Includes index.
  ISBN 0-516-03816-8 ISBN 0-516-26292--0
  1. Kansas—Juvenile literature. I. Fradin, Judith Bloom.
II. Title. III. Series: Fradin, Dennis B. From sea to
shining sea.
F681.3.F73   1995   95-4282
978.1—dc20   CIP
                                                 AC

Table of Contents

University of Kansas band members

INTRODUCING THE SUNFLOWER STATE

Kansas is located in the very center of the United States. Because of this, Kansas is sometimes called "Midway, U.S.A." The "Sunflower State" is Kansas's main nickname. Sunflowers grow wild in much of Kansas. The state was named after the Kansa Indians. *Kansa* means "people of the south wind."

During the 1850s, Kansas was known as "Bleeding Kansas." Bloody battles over slavery were fought there. Later, Kansas was known for its Wild West cattle towns. In the 1870s, Kansas farmers began growing wheat for the whole country.

Today, Kansas leads the states in growing wheat. It also leads the states in making small airplanes. Each year, more visitors come to Kansas. They enjoy the Wild West towns of Wichita, Abilene, and Dodge City.

The Sunflower State is special in other ways. Where was the country's first woman mayor elected? Where was the home of pilot Amelia Earhart? Where did President Dwight Eisenhower grow up? Where did Dorothy of *The Wizard of Oz* live? The answer to these questions is: Kansas!

A picture map of Kansas

Overleaf: Plains wildflowers at Cedar Bluff State Park

5

"Where the Deer and
the Antelope Play"

"Where the Deer and the Antelope Play"

Kansas covers 82,277 square miles of the Midwest. Four states border the Sunflower State. Nebraska is to the north. Missouri is to the east. Oklahoma lies to the south. Colorado is to the west.

Most of the land in Kansas is rather flat. These areas are called plains. They are good for growing wheat and raising cattle. Kansas's plains get higher from east to west. They are also hilly in places. Tall bluffs tower above the plains in other spots. Mount Sunflower is the highest point in the state. It stands 4,039 feet above sea level.

Climate

Kansas has many kinds of weather. On a hot, dry summer day, Kansas can feel like a desert. Summer temperatures often reach 100 degrees Fahrenheit. On a cold, windy winter night, Kansas can feel like the North Pole. Winter temperatures of 10 degrees Fahrenheit are common.

Eastern Kansas gets about 35 inches of rain a year. But far western Kansas averages only 15 inches.

Kansas is the fourteenth-biggest state.

Kings Creek, Konza Prairie Research Natural Area

8

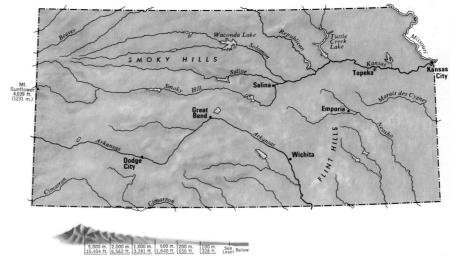

At times, Kansas suffers droughts. These are long spells with little or no rain. Sometimes rain turns into hailstorms. Both drought and hail can damage crops and other property. Kansas has about 18 inches of snowfall each year.

Kansas is known for its windstorms. Only four states are windier than Kansas. Blizzards sometimes hit the state in winter. These snowstorms are driven by high winds. About 40 tornadoes strike Kansas each year. These whirling windstorms are like the one in *The Wizard of Oz.*

Left: Winter at Gardner Lake

The wind speed averages 12.3 miles per hour in Kansas. Only Texas, Florida, and Oklahoma average more tornadoes a year than Kansas.

9

WATERS, WOODS, AND WILDLIFE

The state has about 230 lakes. Many of them were formed by damming rivers. Milford Lake is the largest of these lakes. It covers 25 square miles in northeast Kansas. Also in this part of the state is the Missouri River. It forms the state's northeastern border. The Kansas River flows through northeastern Kansas into the Missouri River. The Arkansas River winds through southern Kansas. Many western Kansas rivers and creeks run dry in the summer.

Kansas has few trees but many grasses. Most of its trees grow along rivers and lakes. The cotton-

A prairie dog mother with her pup

Bluffs and inlet at Elk City Lake, Montgomery County

wood is the state tree. Elms, maples, oaks, and willows grow in Kansas, too. About 200 kinds of grasses grow in Kansas. Bluestem is a tall eastern grass. Buffalo and blue grama are short western grasses. The state flower is the sunflower. It can top 10 feet in height.

"Home on the Range" is the state song. It describes a land "where the deer and the antelope play." Both animals live in Kansas. Prairie dogs, coyotes, badgers, and rattlesnakes are other Kansas animals. Bluegills, bass, and catfish live in the state's rivers and lakes. Hundreds of kinds of birds fill Kansas skies. The western meadowlark is the state bird. Its belly is bright yellow like the state flower.

Left: Bluestem grass
Right: Pomona Lake, Osage County

Pronghorn antelopes are the fastest animals in America. They can top 60 miles per hour. Prairie dogs belong to the squirrel family. Kansas has more prairie chickens than any other state.

11

From Ancient Times Until Today

From Ancient Times Until Today

More than 100 million years ago, seas covered Kansas. Remains of ancient fish and reptiles have been found. Giant lizards called mosasaurs paddled about. Long-necked sea reptiles called plesiosaurs were there, too. Pteranodons flew through the sky. Remains were found of one with a 25-foot wingspan.

About 2 million years ago, the Ice Age began. Glaciers covered northeast Kansas. About 10,000 years ago, the Ice Age ended. The ice masses left behind rich soil.

American Indians

The first people reached Kansas perhaps 15,000 years ago. Ancient human remains were found near Kansas City in 1988. These early Kansans hunted buffalo. They also tracked mammoths. About 1,000 years ago, early Kansas people learned to farm. Some settled down in villages.

By the mid-1500s, several Indian groups lived in Kansas. They included the Kansa (Kaw), Wichita, Osage, and Pawnee. These Indians hunted buffalo,

This partial mosasaur skeleton can be seen at the Sternberg Memorial Museum.

Mammoths were like big, hairy elephants.

Opposite: Settlers from the East on their way to new land in the West

13

antelope, and deer. They grew corn, pumpkins, squash, and beans. The homes of the Kansa and Pawnee were grass-covered log houses called earth lodges. In the early 1600s, Arapaho, Cheyenne, Kiowa, and Comanche groups rode into Kansas. They hunted buffalo from horseback. Their homes were cone-shaped tents made of animal hides. These Indian homes were called tepees.

EUROPEANS AND AMERICANS IN KANSAS

Explorer Francisco Coronado

Francisco Coronado was the first known European explorer in Kansas. He arrived in 1541. Coronado

was searching for gold for Spain. Quivira was said to be a city of gold in Kansas. Instead, it was a Wichita Indian village. Because he didn't find gold there, Coronado left Kansas.

In 1682, France claimed all land drained by the Mississippi River. This included Kansas. French explorers and fur traders arrived in the 1700s. The traders gave pots and beads to the Indians in exchange for furs. In 1744, some French traders built a fort near present-day Leavenworth. But France didn't settle Kansas either.

By 1732, England had thirteen colonies along the Atlantic Ocean. These colonies declared their independence on July 4, 1776. That was the beginning of the United States. The young country soon expanded from the East Coast. In 1803, the United States paid France $15 million for its North American land. This included Kansas.

The first American explorers entered Kansas in 1804. Meriwether Lewis and William Clark traveled along Kansas's northeastern border. Other American explorers went into western Kansas. They described the land as dry and treeless.

Meanwhile, settlers in the eastern United States were seizing Indian lands. The United States government moved these Indians to land unwanted by

Meriwether Lewis

William Clark

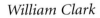

Americans. Kansas was one such place. It was thought to be too dry for farming. About thirty tribes were moved to Kansas. They included the Pottawatomie, Wyandot, and Shawnee. Hardship and disease killed many of these uprooted people.

KANSAS BECOMES A TERRITORY

The Santa Fe Trail opened in 1821. It passed through Kansas on its way from Missouri to New Mexico. In the 1840s, settlers took the Oregon Trail through northern Kansas. Forts were built to protect travelers. Colonel Henry Leavenworth began Fort Leavenworth in 1827. This outpost was Kansas's first permanent non-Indian settlement.

Gold was found in California in 1848. The next year, thousands of gold seekers headed to California. They were nicknamed "forty-niners." Many passed through Kansas. They saw that Kansas had good farmland. Soon there was an outcry to open Kansas for settlement. On May 30, 1854, this was done. The United States government formed the Kansas Territory. Again, the Indians had to move. Most were sent to Oklahoma.

In June 1854, Kansas's first non-Indian town was begun. This was Leavenworth. It was built near

The first territorial capitol, near Junction City

16

A typical Kansas sod house

Fort Leavenworth. Atchison, Topeka, and Lawrence were also begun in 1854. By the next year, nearly 10,000 settlers had come to Kansas. In places with trees, settlers built wooden homes. On the treeless plains, they cut chunks of sod into bricks. With these bricks, they built sod houses.

"BLEEDING KANSAS"

In the 1850s, the South still allowed slavery. It had been outlawed in the North. Many northerners wanted the South to end slavery, too. The Kansas Territory was neither a slave nor a free territory. Rather, Kansans were to decide the matter for themselves. Many people moved to Kansas to settle the slavery question.

On May 21, 1856, proslavery people burned part of Lawrence. John Brown hated slavery. He took revenge two nights later. Brown led an antislavery raid. His forces murdered five proslavery men along the Pottawatomie Creek.

To some, John Brown was a hero. Others called him a mad killer. His deed sparked more fights over

Left: John Brown
Right: Antislavery Kansas "free-staters" preparing for battle

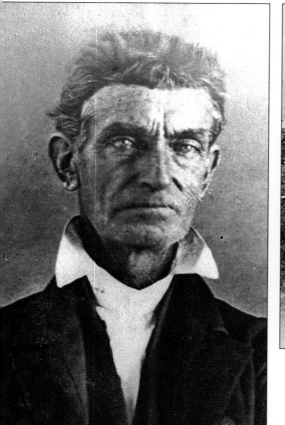

slavery. About 50 people were killed. The area became known as "Bleeding Kansas." Kansans, called Jayhawkers, made raids into Missouri. Missouri was a slave state. The Jayhawkers freed Missouri slaves and attacked slaveholders.

Yet, fighting did not decide Kansas's slavery question. Voting did. In 1859, Kansans voted on a constitution. It outlawed slavery.

STATEHOOD AND CIVIL WAR

Kansas had well over 100,000 people by 1861. That January 29, it became the thirty-fourth state. Dr. Charles Robinson was Kansas's first state governor. Topeka became the state capital.

In April, the Civil War (1861-1865) began. The Union (the North) fought the Confederacy (the South). More than 20,000 Kansans fought for the Union. Among them were 2,000 black Kansans.

Many people in Kansas died during Confederate raids. On August 21, 1863, William Quantrill led a raid into Lawrence. The raiders killed 180 men and boys and burned the town. The Battle of Mine Creek was the state's largest Civil War clash. The Union won this battle. The Union won the war in 1865. The North's victory freed all slaves.

Governor Charles Robinson

Of all the states, Kansas sent the largest percentage of its men to the Union army.

19

The Atchison, Topeka & Santa Fe Railroad station in Nortonville

RAILROADS, CATTLE TOWNS, AND WHEAT FARMS

Congress had passed the Homestead Act in 1862. It offered free land to people who settled in the West. After the war, many people claimed homesteads in Kansas. The state's population swelled to 365,000 by 1870.

Railroads were built in Kansas after the war. The Union Pacific Railroad reached Denver from Kansas City by 1870. By 1872, the famous Atchison, Topeka & Santa Fe Railroad stretched across Kansas. Trains brought more people to the state. They also helped build cattle towns in Kansas.

Cattle trails were blazed from Texas to Kansas. Cowboys on horseback drove cattle north along the trails. Wichita and Abilene were Kansas towns on the Chisholm Trail. Dodge City was on the Western Trail. From these cattle towns, the animals went by train to eastern cities. From 1875 to 1885, Dodge City was a giant cattle market. People called it the "Cowboy Capital of the World."

Kansas's cattle towns were wild places. Fistfights and gun battles broke out in the streets and saloons. Many lawmen tried to tame these towns. Wild Bill Hickok was marshal of Abilene. Wyatt Earp and Bat Masterson were Dodge City lawmen.

The Texas-to-Kansas cattle drives ended around 1885. Kansans began to raise their own cattle. By

Wild Bill Hickok

Cowboys with a herd of cattle near Ashland

then, they were also growing huge wheat crops. Mennonites from Russia had come to central Kansas in 1874. They brought with them Turkey Red wheat. It grew well in Kansas. Kansas led the country at growing wheat by the early 1900s. Flour mills were built in Kansas to grind the wheat. Many Americans ate bread made from Kansas wheat. The state became known as the "Breadbasket of America."

By the early 1900s, Kansas was also a mining state. Coal was mined in the southeast. Oil and natural gas also came from the southeast.

World Wars, Depression, and Segregation

In 1917, the United States entered World War I (1914-1918). Training camps were set up at Camp Funston and Fort Leavenworth. More than 80,000 Kansans served in the war. Kansas wheat and cattle also helped win the war.

The Great Depression (1929-1939) brought hard times to the whole country. Prices for crops fell. Many Kansas farmers lost their farms. Businesses, banks, and mines closed in Kansas. Then, drought struck in 1931. Crops died. Winds lifted the dry soil. This started dust storms called black blizzards.

Alf Landon was Kansas's governor (1933-1937) during most of the depression. He ran for president in 1936. But Landon lost to President Franklin D. Roosevelt. F.D.R. had begun many public works programs. They helped Americans through the depression. Kansans got jobs building schools and roads. They also planted trees.

In 1941, the United States entered World War II (1939-1945). Nearly half the country's B-29 warplanes were made in Wichita. About 215,000 Kansas men and women served in the war. General Dwight "Ike" Eisenhower played a key role in winning the war. He grew up in Abilene.

Much of southern Kansas was part of the "Dust Bowl." This area had very bad dust storms.

General Eisenhower returned from the war a hero. In 1952, "Ike" ran for president of the United States. In 1953, the man from the thirty-fourth state became the thirty-fourth president.

In the 1950s, many United States cities had segregated schools. Black children and white children went to separate schools. In 1950, Oliver Brown sued the Topeka Board of Education. His daughter Linda had been turned away at a white school. This school was closer to their home. In 1954, the United States Supreme Court made an important ruling. It is called *Brown vs. Board of Education of Topeka.* The ruling said that schoolchildren must not be segregated by race. This case paved the way for United States schools to be integrated.

Keeping the races apart is called segregation. Bringing them together is called integration.

RECENT PROBLEMS AND SUCCESSES

Kansas faces several problems. Farm goods are sold at low prices. Yet, farmers must pay high prices for supplies. Thousands of farmers have been forced out of business. Many small Kansas farming towns have died. Two of every three Kansans now live in cities. Big-city problems have come with this. Wichita, Kansas City, and Topeka suffer from crime, gangs, and drugs.

Kansas's aquifers are another important matter. They provide water for crops, cattle, and cities. Some of these underground water supplies have become polluted. Farm chemicals and factory wastes have leaked into them. The Ogallala aquifer is a major source of water in Kansas. By 1982, Kansans had used one-third of the Ogallala's water.

Yet, Kansas has much to be proud of. Its meat-packing and natural-gas industries have expanded. Garden City has the world's largest meat-packing plant. It opened in 1980. In 1990, Kansas grew a record wheat crop. A 1994 study honored the state as one of the five best states in which to live.

An old barn in a sorghum field near Centralia

An aquifer is an underground source of water.

Overleaf: Boys playing soccer, Johnson County

25

Kansans and Their Work

KANSANS AND THEIR WORK

Kansans love their state and their hometowns. "The proudest thing I can claim is that I am from Abilene," said President Eisenhower. Or as Dorothy said as she returned from Oz: "There's no place like home!"

Kansas has about 2.5 million people. About nine of every ten Kansans are white. Most of their ancestors came from Germany, Ireland, and England. After the Civil War, thousands of black settlers came to Kansas. They built several towns, including Nicodemus. Today, there are almost 150,000 black people in Kansas. Almost 100,000 Hispanics live in Kansas. Most of their families came from Mexico. About 35,000 Kansans have Asian backgrounds. Another 22,000 are American Indians. The Pottawatomie are now the state's largest tribe.

Plains Indians in costume about to participate in a Nicodemus parade

KANSANS AT WORK

About half of all Kansans have jobs. About 260,000 of the state's 1.3 million workers sell goods. Another 260,000 of the state's workers provide services. This group includes lawyers and health-care

Assembly-line check at the Learjet plant in Wichita

Electronic technicians doing precision alignment of aircraft radio equipment at a company in Olathe

workers. The Menninger Clinic is a famous mental-health center. It's in Topeka.

Kansas has nearly 250,000 government workers. They include teachers and workers at prisons and military bases. McConnell Air Force Base is near Wichita. Leavenworth Prison is part of the fort.

Nearly 200,000 Kansans make goods. Kansas is a leading maker of airplanes and airplane parts. The giant Boeing Company makes airplane parts in Wichita. Automobiles are also made in Kansas. Foods are the state's second-leading product. These include flour, meat, and animal feed. About 70,000 Kansans work in communications and related fields. Sprint is a big long-distance telephone company. It is based in Overland Park.

Kansas has about 65,000 farms and ranches. Farms cover 75,000 square miles. That is nine-tenths of the state's land. Only Texas and Montana have more farmland. About 23 billion pounds of wheat are harvested in Kansas each year. That is more than the amount grown by any other state. Most Kansas wheat is used to make bread. Some is used in breakfast cereals. Kansas leads the country at growing sorghum. This grain is used as animal feed. Kansas and Nebraska are often tied for second place at raising beef cattle. Only Texas raises more.

Another 10,000 Kansans work in mining. Kansas ranks sixth in the country at mining natural gas. This is used for cooking and heating. Kansas is the country's top helium producer. Helium is used in rockets and scientific balloons. Kansas is a major oil-producing state. Other mining products are stone, salt, sand, and gravel.

An oil well in a wheat field near Geneseo

Overleaf: Elk Falls, on the Elk River

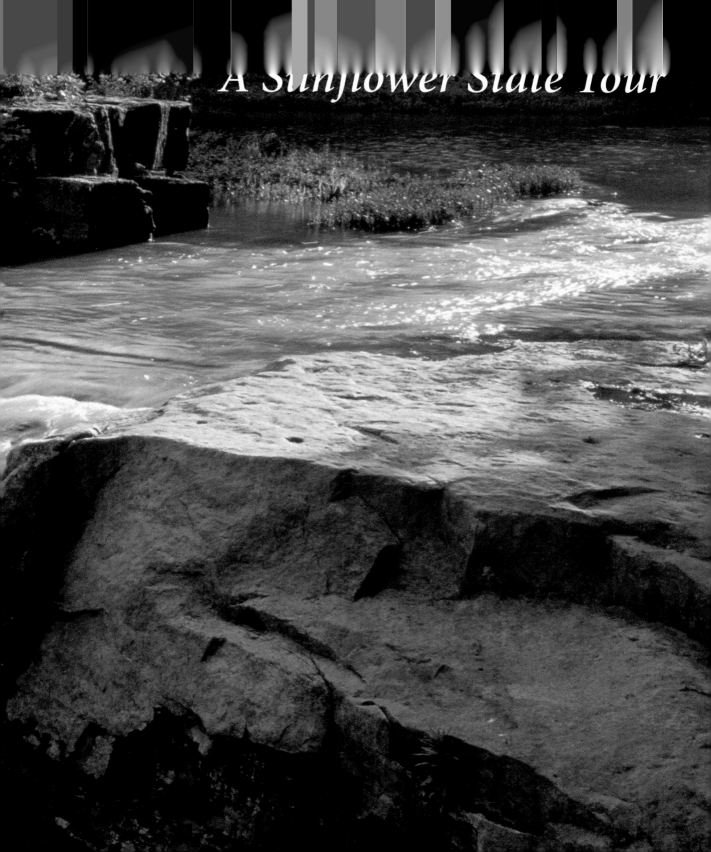

A Sunflower State Tour

A SUNFLOWER STATE TOUR

Kansas towns honor their Indian, farming, and cowboy histories. Visitors to the state's larger cities enjoy art and science museums. Others soak up the sunshine under Kansas's blue skies.

NORTHEASTERN KANSAS

Another Kansas City lies just to the east in Missouri.

Kansas City lies where the Missouri and Kansas rivers meet. It is called the "Gateway to Kansas." The city was begun by Wyandot Indians in 1843. Today, Kansas City is the state's second-largest city. About 150,000 people live there. It is also a great flour-milling and meat-packing center.

The Grinter House is Kansas City's oldest home. Moses Grinter built it in 1856. The Children's Museum of Kansas City offers science and art activities. There, children can learn how airplanes fly. Some visitors enjoy cruises on the *Missouri River Queen*. This is a paddle-wheel steamboat.

Bonner Springs is outside Kansas City. It is the home of the Agricultural Hall of Fame. The

American farmer is honored there. Visitors can see America's largest collection of farm tools and machinery. Young visitors can do farm chores that children did 100 years ago.

Leavenworth is north of Kansas City. The Leavenworth County Museum is in a sixteen-room mansion. Visitors there see how well-to-do people lived in the 1800s. North of the city is Fort Leavenworth. Begun in 1827, this army post is still in use. Visitors enjoy the Post Museum. It has the country's largest collection of horse-drawn vehicles.

Atchison is farther north. The Amelia Earhart Birthplace is there. Visitors can see the bedroom

A one-room schoolhouse display at the Agricultural Hall of Fame in Bonner Springs

Strong Hall,
University of Kansas

The Pioneer Woman
statue

where Earhart was born. Earhart became a famous airplane pilot. Forest of Friendship is near Atchison. Plaques there honor people who advanced aviation. The forest was begun by the Ninety-nines. This is a group of women pilots. Earhart helped found the group in 1929.

Lawrence is west of Kansas City. The University of Kansas (KU) is there. With more than 29,000 students, it is the state's largest school. KU's Dyche Museum of Natural History has plesiosaur and pteranodon fossils. KU is also known for its sports teams. The Jayhawks have won several track and basketball titles.

Topeka is west of Lawrence. Founded in 1854, it is now the state's third-biggest city. About 120,000 people live there. Topeka has been the state capital since 1861. Kansas lawmakers meet at the State Capitol. The *Pioneer Woman* statue is on the capitol grounds. It was made by Topekan sculptor Merrell Gage. Inside the capitol are murals of Kansas life and history. Kansas artist John Steuart Curry created two of them. The Kansas Museum of History is also in Topeka. Children like its 1880 train and a replica of an Oregon Trail wagon.

Manhattan is west of Topeka. Kansas State University is there. The college runs nearby Konza

Prairie. This 15-square-mile grassland shows the way Kansas looked before settlers came. A herd of nearly 200 buffalo lives at Konza Prairie.

Fort Riley is west of Manhattan. About 15,000 soldiers are stationed there. This fort is Kansas's biggest military base. George Custer was once stationed there. He died later fighting Indians in Montana. George Patton also served at Fort Riley. He helped win World War II in Europe.

Junction City is near Fort Riley. The Kansas Vietnam Memorial is there. It honors the nearly 800 Kansans killed in the Vietnam War (1964-1973).

The Kansas Vietnam Memorial

Left: This statue of Dwight D. Eisenhower can be seen at the Eisenhower Center in Abilene.
Right: An aerial view of Wichita

Abilene is a short drive west of Junction City. The Eisenhower Center is there. It includes President Dwight Eisenhower's boyhood home. His piano and schoolbooks can be seen there. Salina is west of Abilene. Its Smoky Hill Museum has Indian and pioneer exhibits. One museum room looks like an 1880s general store.

SOUTHEASTERN HIGHLIGHTS

Country Critters is in Burlington. This is the world's largest maker of puppets. Many stuffed animals are also made there. Visitors to the company can watch how puppets are made. To the southeast is the Fort Scott National Historic Site. This fort was built in 1842. It has been restored. Visitors can learn about a frontier soldier's life.

Drummers at the Fort Scott National Historic Site

Chanute is southwest of the fort. It is home to the Martin and Osa Johnson Safari Museum. The Johnsons traveled the world between 1917 and 1936. They made movies of people and wildlife. One airplane they flew in was painted to look like a giraffe. The museum displays their many photographs.

Coffeyville is south of Chanute. Visitors can learn about three outlaw brothers at the Dalton Museum. The brothers were Bob, Grat, and Emmett Dalton. On October 5, 1892, with two others, they tried to rob two Coffeyville banks at once. Townspeople stopped them in a big gun battle. Bob and Grat and two others were killed. Four townsmen were also killed. Emmett was wounded. He spent fourteen years in jail.

Wichita is northwest of Coffeyville. It lies on the Arkansas and Little Arkansas rivers. Long ago, the Wichita Indians lived there. The town was settled in 1864. Today, Wichita is the state's biggest city. More than 300,000 people live there. Many airplanes and airplane parts are made in Wichita.

Old Cowtown Museum is in Wichita. It has more than thirty buildings from the 1870s. Wichita's first house and jail are there. So is a one-room school. The Mid-America All-Indian Center and Museum is also in Wichita. It shows American Indian history and arts and crafts. A 44-foot-tall statue of an Indian guards the grounds. It is called *Keeper of the Plains.* The Children's Museum invites visitors to "Please Touch." It holds puppet and science shows. Wichita's Sedgwick County Zoo is noted for its bears, chimps, and snakes.

The Keeper of the Plains *statue (left) is on the grounds of the Mid-America All-Indian Center and Museum in Wichita (right).*

Northwest of Wichita is Hutchinson. Many people enjoy its Kansas Cosmosphere and Space Center. It has the world's biggest space-suit collection. Real spacecraft can be seen there, too. The Kansas State Fairgrounds is also in Hutchinson. The State Fair is held there each September.

An exhibit at the Kansas Cosmosphere and Space Center

SOUTHWEST KANSAS

Southwest Kansas has no big cities. It does have many farms, ranches, and small towns. Pratt is west of Wichita. The Pratt County Historical Museum is

A street in Old Dodge City

there. Its "Old-Time Main Street" shows how the state's small towns looked in the 1890s.

Greensburg is west of Pratt. About 2,000 years ago, a meteorite struck the earth near present-day Greensburg. The giant Pallasite Meteorite was found in 1949. Later, it was moved to Greensburg. The meteorite weighs about 1,000 pounds.

Dodge City is west of Greensburg. Visitors can walk down Historic Front Street. It looks like the town's main street of the 1870s. At the Boot Hill Museum, visitors learn about Dodge City's colorful past. Gunfighters and cowboys were buried at nearby Boot Hill Cemetery. Now each summer, cowboys take part in the town's rodeos. Today, Dodge City is home to the Kansas Teacher's Hall of Fame. It honors outstanding Kansas teachers.

The town of Liberal is in Kansas's southwest corner. Dorothy's House stands there. It looks just like the house in the movie *The Wizard of Oz*. The Land of Oz is behind the house. There, visitors can meet the Cowardly Lion and the Wizard.

Garden City is north of Liberal. The Finney County Wildlife Area is south of town. Visitors spot deer, badgers, quail, and coyotes. A herd of about sixty buffalo also roams about.

Northeast of Garden City are Ness City and Beeler. George Washington Carver lived outside Ness City (1888-1891). Later, he earned great fame as a scientist. A roadside marker shows where his farm once stood. A museum in Beeler honors this black American.

NORTHWEST KANSAS

George Washington Carver said that oil would be found in western Kansas. His words came true. Northwest Kansas has few people but many oil wells. Hill City is in the middle of northwestern Kansas. The Historical Oil Museum is at Hill City.

There, visitors learn about past and present ways of finding oil.

Hays is south of Hill City. The Ellis County Historical Museum is in Hays. The museum is in an 1873 church. It shows furniture and farm machinery from the county's past. The Sternberg Museum is also in Hays. A fossil of an 80-million-year-old fish is displayed there. Inside this fish is the fossil of another fish. This is called the fish within a fish.

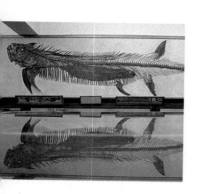

The fish-within-a-fish fossil at the Sternberg Museum

West of Hays stands 70-foot-tall Castle Rock. It looks like an old castle. Farther west is Monument Rocks National Landmark. Tall pyramid-shaped rocks are there. West of Monument Rocks is Oakley. Its Fick Fossil Museum has over 11,000 shark teeth. North of Oakley is Prairie Dog Town. Visitors can feed tame deer, raccoons, foxes, and prairie dogs.

Colby and Goodland are west of Hill City. The Prairie Museum of Art and History is in Colby. On its grounds, visitors can enter a sod house. They can also explore a 1930s farm. America's first helicopter was built in Goodland in 1910. Goodland's High Plains Museum has a replica of it. The museum also has displays about Indian and pioneer life.

Norton is north of Hill City. It is near the state's northern border. The Presidential Also-Ran

Gallery is there. It honors people who ran for president but lost.

Athol is east of Norton. The restored Home on the Range Cabin is north of town. There, Dr. Brewster Higley wrote the words to "Home on the Range." In 1947, it became the state song.

Lebanon is east of Athol. It is a good place to end a Kansas tour. The Geographic Center Marker is outside Lebanon. Anyone standing there is in the middle of the United States. That's not counting Alaska and Hawaii.

*Left: Castle Rock
Right: Keyhole Arch at Monument Rocks National Landmark*

Daniel Kelley, who lived in nearby Harlan, wrote the music for "Home on the Range."

Overleaf: President Dwight David Eisenhower

43

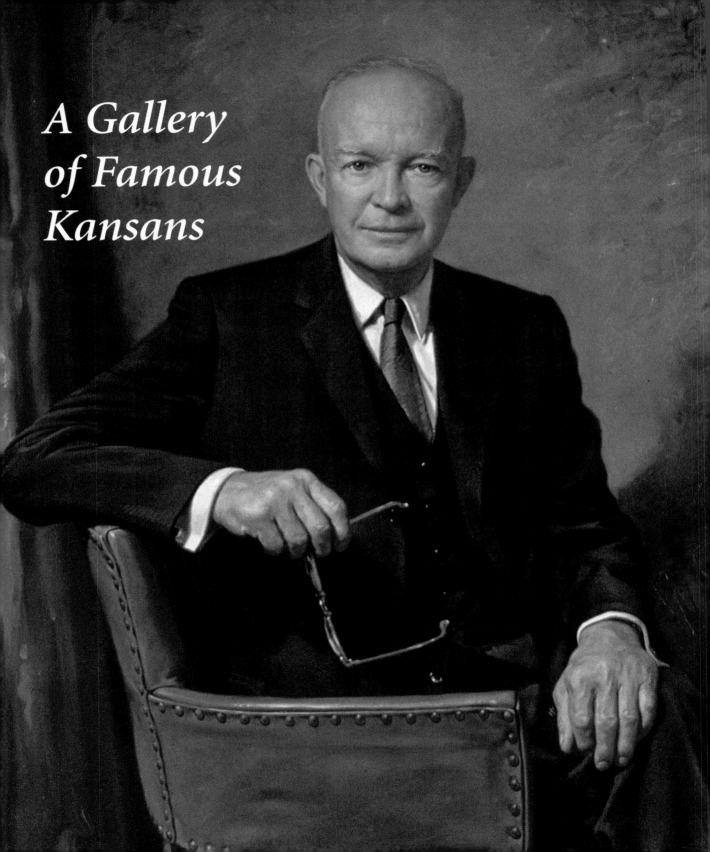

A Gallery
of Famous
Kansans

A GALLERY OF FAMOUS KANSANS

Carry Nation

Many great Americans have come from Kansas. They include athletes, authors, and lawmakers.

Carry Nation (1846-1911) was born in Kentucky. She moved to Kansas in 1889. She lived in Medicine Lodge with her second husband, Reverend David Nation. Her first husband drank himself to death. In 1880, Kansans had outlawed liquor. Many saloons still sold it. In 1899, Nation began attacking saloons. She broke bottles with her hatchet. Nation also did this in other states. Today, someone who strongly opposes liquor is called a "Carry Nation."

Charles Curtis (1860-1936) was part Kansa Indian. He was born on Indian land that is now part of Topeka. Curtis served Kansas in the U.S. House of Representatives (1893-1907) and Senate (1907-1913 and 1915-1929). Curtis was also vice president of the United States (1929-1933).

Robert Dole was born in Russell in 1923. He was wounded during World War II. Dole lost the use of his right arm. Since 1969, he has represented Kansas in the U.S. Senate. There, he served as

Nancy Kassebaum

Karl Menninger

floor leader (1985-1987 and 1995-). **Nancy Landon Kassebaum** was born in Topeka in 1932. Her father was Alf Landon. Kassebaum has been Kansas's other U.S. senator since 1978. In 1994, she was named to chair the Senate Labor Committee. Kassebaum is the first woman to head a major Senate committee.

In 1925, two Topeka doctors opened a clinic in a farmhouse. They were **Charles Menninger** (1862-1953) and his son **Karl Menninger** (1893-1990). These men wanted to help mentally ill people. Karl's brother, **William Claire Menninger** (1899-1966), soon joined them. Their clinic became a famous mental-health center.

Earl Sutherland (1915-1974) was born in Burlingame. He became a doctor and a scientist. In 1956, he learned how hormones affect the human body. Dr. Sutherland won the 1971 Nobel Prize in medicine for his work. **Wes Jackson** was born on the family farm near Topeka in 1936. He studied plants, soil, and farming. Jackson began the Land Institute near Salina. People there study how to plant crops that save the soil.

Walter Chrysler (1875-1940) was born in Wamego. In 1924, he built the first Chrysler car. His Chrysler Corporation became a giant automaker.

Amelia Earhart (1897-1937) was born in Atchison. In her twenties, she learned to fly a plane. In 1932, Earhart flew across the Atlantic Ocean alone. She was the first woman to do that. In 1935, she flew from Honolulu, Hawaii, to the American mainland. She was the first person ever to do that alone. Two years later, Earhart disappeared over the Pacific. She was trying to fly around the world.

Amelia Earhart

Dorothy Canfield Fisher

Gordon Parks

Aaron Douglas (1899-1979) was born in Topeka. He painted murals about black life. He also illustrated many books. Some were written by such black authors as Langston Hughes and James Weldon Johnson.

Many writers have been Kansans. **William Allen White** (1868-1944) was born in Emporia. He published and wrote for the *Emporia Gazette*. Newspapers across the country quoted his columns. White was called the "Sage of Emporia." He won the 1923 Pulitzer Prize for editorial writing. **Dorothy Canfield Fisher** (1879-1958) was born in Lawrence. She wrote more than sixty books for children and adults. *Understood Betsy* is a novel for young people. It tells about a city girl learning about life on a family farm.

Damon Runyon (1880-1946) was born in Manhattan. By the age of fifteen, he was a newspaper reporter. Runyon became a sportswriter and story writer. He also wrote the 1934 movie *Little Miss Marker*. The musical *Guys and Dolls* was based on his stories. **Rex Stout** (1886-1975) was born in Indiana. He grew up in Wakarusa. Stout was the Kansas state spelling champ at age thirteen. He worked as a cook for a while. Then, he wrote mystery stories. In them, Nero Wolfe was an overweight detective. *Too Many Cooks* was one of Stout's Nero Wolfe mysteries.

Gordon Parks was born in Fort Scott in 1912. He became a writer, photographer, and composer. His best-known novel is *The Learning Tree*. It is about growing up black in Kansas. Parks directed the movie made from this novel. He was Hollywood's first major black director. **William Inge** (1913-1973) was born in Independence. He became a great playwright. *Picnic* is about a handsome stranger in a Kansas town. It won the 1953 Pulitzer Prize in drama.

Two Kansans became famous poets. **Edgar Lee Masters** (1868-1950) was born in Garnett. His best-known work is *Spoon River Anthology*. Through several poems, it tells the stories of small-town people. **Gwendolyn Brooks** was born in Topeka in 1917. She published her first poems at age thirteen. *Annie Allen* is a book of verses. It won the 1950 Pulitzer Prize in poetry.

Eva Jessye (1895-1992) was born in Coffeyville. She entered college at age thirteen. Jessye became a choral director, actress, and composer. In 1929, she directed the Eva Jessye Choir in *Hallelujah*. This was the first black movie musical. Kansas held "Eva Jessye Day" in 1978.

Edgar Lee Masters

Gwendolyn Brooks

Charlie "Bird" Parker

Vivian Vance

Charlie "Bird" Parker (1920-1955) was born in Kansas City. When he was thirteen, his mother bought him a saxophone. Later, "Bird" played with some great jazz bands. He helped create a kind of jazz. It's called bebop. "Cherokee" and "Koko" are among his recordings.

Some fine actors have also come from Kansas. **Hattie McDaniel** (1895-1952) was born in Wichita. She appeared in nearly eighty movies. In 1939, she won an Academy Award. It was for best supporting actress in *Gone With the Wind*. McDaniel was the first black American to win an Academy Award. **Buster Keaton** (1895-1966) was born in Piqua. He became a great comedian in silent movies. Keaton was called the "Great Stone Face." *The General* is one of his best-known films. **Vivian Vance** (1912-1979) was born in Cherryvale. She played Ethel Mertz on television's "I Love Lucy." **Ed Asner** was born in Kansas City in 1929. He is best known as television's Lou Grant. **Dennis Hopper** was born in Dodge City in 1936. He saw his first movie at the age of five. That's when he decided to become an actor. His movies include *Easy Rider, Hoosiers,* and *Speed*.

Kansas has also produced many athletes. **Jess Willard** (1881-1968) was born in Pottawatomie

County. At first he was a cowboy. When he was about twenty-seven, Willard started boxing. "Cowboy Jess" won the heavyweight title in 1915. He was champion until 1919.

Two Baseball Hall of Famers were Kansans. **Joe Tinker** (1880-1948) was born in Muscotah. He became a great Chicago Cubs shortstop. He was part of the "Tinker to Evers to Chance" double-play combination. Four times, he led National League shortstops in fielding. **Walter "Big Train" Johnson** (1887-1946) was born in Humboldt. He was the fastest pitcher ever. Johnson won 416 games. The "Big Train" holds the shutout record with 110. Johnson was elected to the Baseball Hall of Fame in 1936. Ten years later, Tinker made it.

Glenn Cunningham (1900-1988) was born in Atlanta, Kansas. When he was seven, his legs were badly burned. Doctors feared he would never walk. But the "Kansas Ironman" became a great runner. Cunningham won a silver medal in the 1936 Olympics. It was for the 1,500-meter run. He and his wife later opened the Glenn Cunningham Youth Ranch near Wichita. Over thirty years, they cared for 10,000 foster children.

Jim Ryun was born in 1947 in Wichita. He couldn't make his freshman track team. Ryun began

Joe Tinker

Gale Sayers

Barry Sanders

running 5 miles a day through Wichita's streets. At age seventeen, Ryun ran the mile in under four minutes. He became the first high-school student to do that. The "Stork in Shorts" won a silver medal in the 1968 Olympics. It was for the 1,500-meter run.

Lynette Woodard was born in Wichita in 1959. She became a University of Kansas basketball star. In her second year, Woodard led the country in scoring. She averaged thirty-one points a game. Woodard was captain of the 1984 U.S. Olympic team. It won America's first gold medal in women's basketball. In 1985, Woodard became the Harlem Globetrotter's first woman player.

Pro football players have been Kansans, too. **Gale Sayers** was born in Wichita in 1943. He played for the Chicago Bears. In one game, he scored a record six touchdowns. Sayers was voted the best running back in pro football's first fifty years. **John Riggins** was born in Centralia in 1949. Riggins set an NFL record by scoring twenty-four touchdowns in one season. Both Sayers and Riggins are in the Pro Football Hall of Fame. **Barry Sanders** was born in Wichita in 1968. He is one of football's brightest stars today. In 1994, he led the NFL in yards gained. Sanders gained 1,883 yards.

Lynette Woodard

The birthplace of Glenn Cunningham, Robert Dole, Eva Jessye, and Amelia Earhart . . .

Home also to Dwight Eisenhower, Carry Nation, Rex Stout, and Charles Menninger . . .

The top producer of wheat and helium, and a leader in beef cattle and airplanes . . .

Site of the geographic center of the United States . . .

This is the Sunflower State—Kansas!

Did You Know?

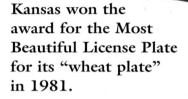

Lawrin, the horse that won the 1938 Kentucky Derby, was born in Kansas.

The name *Topeka* is an Indian word that means "good place to dig potatoes."

Millions of children draw with Crayolas. The Binney-Smith Crayon Company, based in Winfield, makes 5 million Crayola crayons a day.

Kansans honor their state with a holiday. January 29, the state's birthday, is Kansas Day. Schoolchildren sing Kansas songs. They also do projects on Kansas history for this special day.

Deborah Irene Bryant of Overland Park was Miss America in 1966. Debra Dene Barnes of Moran held the title in 1968.

Kansas won the award for the Most Beautiful License Plate for its "wheat plate" in 1981.

One of the world's largest balls of twine was begun by a farmer at Cawker City. Each year, Cawker City people hold a twine-a-thon at which they add to the giant ball of string. By 1995, it weighed about 17,000 pounds and was still growing.

Emmett Kelly, one of the most famous circus clowns of all time, was born in Sedan.

In 1920, Tom Henry of Arkansas City invented a candy bar called the Tom Henry. Later, it became the famous Oh Henry! bar.

Kansans live about seventy-six years on average. Only in a handful of other states do people live longer.

Kansas claims to be the home of horseshoe pitching. In 1909, Bronson hosted the country's first international horseshoe pitching contest.

Kansan Susanna Madora Salter (1860-1961) was the first woman mayor of a United States town. She was elected mayor of Argonia in 1887. Salter served one year and earned one dollar.

Almon Strowger of El Dorado invented the dial telephone in 1889.

Dodge City is the country's second-windiest city. Wind speeds there average 14 miles per hour.

The largest hailstone in the United States fell at Coffeyville in 1970. The giant ice lump was 17.5 inches around. It weighed 1.66 pounds.

Kansas has towns named Bird City, Admire, Pretty Prairie, Buffalo, Green, and Gas.

Kansas's first newspaper, the *Shawnee Sun*, was published in the Shawnee Indian language in 1835.

A farmer near Greensburg was one of the few people to look up inside a tornado and survive. In 1928, Will Keller was about to enter his storm cellar when a tornado appeared overhead. "A screaming hissing sound came from the end of the funnel," he later said. "The walls of the opening were of rotating clouds made visible by zigzagging flashes of lightning."

Clyde Tombaugh, who grew up in Burdett, discovered the planet Pluto in 1930.

Kansas Information

State flag

Sunflowers

Western meadowlark

Area: 82,277 square miles (the fourteenth-biggest state)

Greatest Distance North to South: 206 miles

Greatest Distance East to West: 408 miles

Border States: Nebraska to the north; Missouri to the east; Oklahoma to the south; Colorado to the west

Highest Point: Mount Sunflower in the northwest, 4,039 feet above sea level

Lowest Point: Along the Verdigris River in the southeast, 680 feet above sea level

Hottest Recorded Temperature: 121° F. (on July 18, 1936, at Fredonia, and on July 24, 1936, near Alton)

Coldest Recorded Temperature: -40° F. (on February 13, 1905, at Lebanon)

Statehood: The thirty-fourth state, on January 29, 1861

Origin of Name: Kansas means "people of the south wind" in the Kansa Indian language

Capital: Topeka

Counties: 105

United States Senators: 2

United States Representatives: 4

State Senators: 40

State Representatives: 125

State Song: "Home on the Range," by Dr. Brewster Higley (words) and Daniel Kelley (music)

State March: "The Kansas March," by Duff E. Middleton

State Motto: *Ad Astra per Aspera* (Latin, meaning "To the Stars Through Difficulties")

Nicknames: "Sunflower State," "Jayhawker State," "Breadbasket of America," "Midway, U.S.A.," "Wheat State"

State Seal: Adopted in 1861

State Flag: Adopted in 1925; modified in 1927 and 1961

State Flower: Sunflower

State Bird: Western meadowlark

State Tree: Cottonwood

State Animal: Buffalo

State Reptile: Ornate box turtle

State Insect: Honeybee

Some Rivers: Missouri, Arkansas, Kansas, Republican, Solomon, Saline, Smoky Hill, Neosho, Verdigris, Cimarron

Some Lakes: Milford, Tuttle Creek, Wilson, John Redmond, Elk City, Perry

Wildlife: Deer, pronghorns, coyotes, prairie dogs, badgers, foxes, rabbits, raccoons, western meadowlarks, prairie chickens, pheasants, quails, owls, woodpeckers, cardinals, blue jays, robins, many other kinds of birds, rattlesnakes, copperheads, many nonpoisonous snakes, catfish, bluegills, bass, crappies

Manufactured Products: Airplanes, airplane parts, missiles, automobiles, other transportation equipment, packaged meat, flour, animal feed, medicine, chemicals, books, clothing

Farm Products: Wheat, beef cattle, hay, sorghum, corn, soybeans, hogs, milk, oats, barley, sugar beets

Mining: Natural gas, helium, oil, salt, coal, crushed stone

Population: 2,477,574, thirty-second among the states (1990 U.S. Census Bureau figures)

Major Cities (1990 Census):

Wichita	304,011	Olathe	63,352
Kansas City	149,767	Salina	42,303
Topeka	119,883	Hutchinson	39,308
Overland Park	111,790	Leavenworth	38,495
Lawrence	65,608	Shawnee	37,993

Cottonwood tree

Box turtle

Honeybees

Kansas History

An Osage Indian couple outside their grass house

About 13,000 B.C.—The first people reach Kansas

About A.D. 1000—Indians in Kansas begin to farm

1541—Francisco Coronado, a Spanish explorer, is the first European in Kansas

1682—France claims all land drained by the Mississippi River, including Kansas

1764—French fur trade with the Indians becomes organized

1776—The United States declares independence from England

1803—The United States buys all French land in North America, including Kansas

1804—American explorers Meriwether Lewis and William Clark enter Kansas on their way to the Pacific Northwest

1806—Lewis and Clark reenter Kansas on their return trip; American explorer Zebulon Pike travels across Kansas

1820s-1840s—The U.S. government moves about thirty Indian tribes to Kansas from other parts of the country

1827—Fort Leavenworth, the first permanent non-Indian settlement in Kansas, is begun

1835—Kansas's first newspaper, the *Shawnee Sun,* is printed in the Shawnee Indian language near present-day Kansas City

1854—The Kansas Territory is created, forcing Indians to move and opening the land to settlers

1856—Kansas becomes known as "Bleeding Kansas" after proslavery and antislavery groups lead bloody raids

1859—Kansas approves a constitution that outlaws slavery

1861—On January 29, Kansas becomes the thirty-fourth state

1861-65—Kansas sends more than 20,000 men to help the North win the Civil War and end slavery in the South

1874—A Mennonite colony from Russia introduces Turkey Red wheat to Kansas

1875-85—Dodge City is one of the world's great cattle markets

1887—Kansas women are given the right to vote in town elections; Susanna Madora Salter of Argonia is elected the first woman mayor of a U.S. town

1892—Oil is discovered near Neodesha in southeast Kansas

1903—Helium is discovered in Dexter in southeast Kansas

1912—Kansas women gain their complete voting rights

1917-18—Kansas provides more than 80,000 troops to help win World War I

1928—Kansan Charles Curtis is elected vice president of the United States

1929-39—The Great Depression hurts farming and industry in Kansas and in the rest of the nation

1936—Kansas governor Alf Landon runs for president of the United States but loses to President Franklin D. Roosevelt

1941-45—About 215,000 Kansas men and women help win World War II

1952—Dwight Eisenhower of Abilene is elected thirty-fourth president of the United States

1954—The U.S. Supreme Court rules in *Brown vs. Board of Education of Topeka* that segregated schools are illegal

1958—One of the country's first civil-rights "sit-ins" is held in Wichita, resulting in black people being allowed to be served at a drugstore lunch counter

1961—The Sunflower State is 100 years old on January 29

1978—Nancy Landon Kassebaum is elected to the U.S. Senate, becoming the first woman senator elected on her own for a full term

1990—The state's population nears 2.5 million; Kansas grows a record wheat crop

1991—Joan Finney becomes that state's first woman governor; a tornado kills seventeen people in Kansas

1994—Kansas grows its largest corn crop in history

1995—Two Kansas natives—Robert Dole and Arlen Specter—enter the race for the Republican presidential nomination

Alf Landon

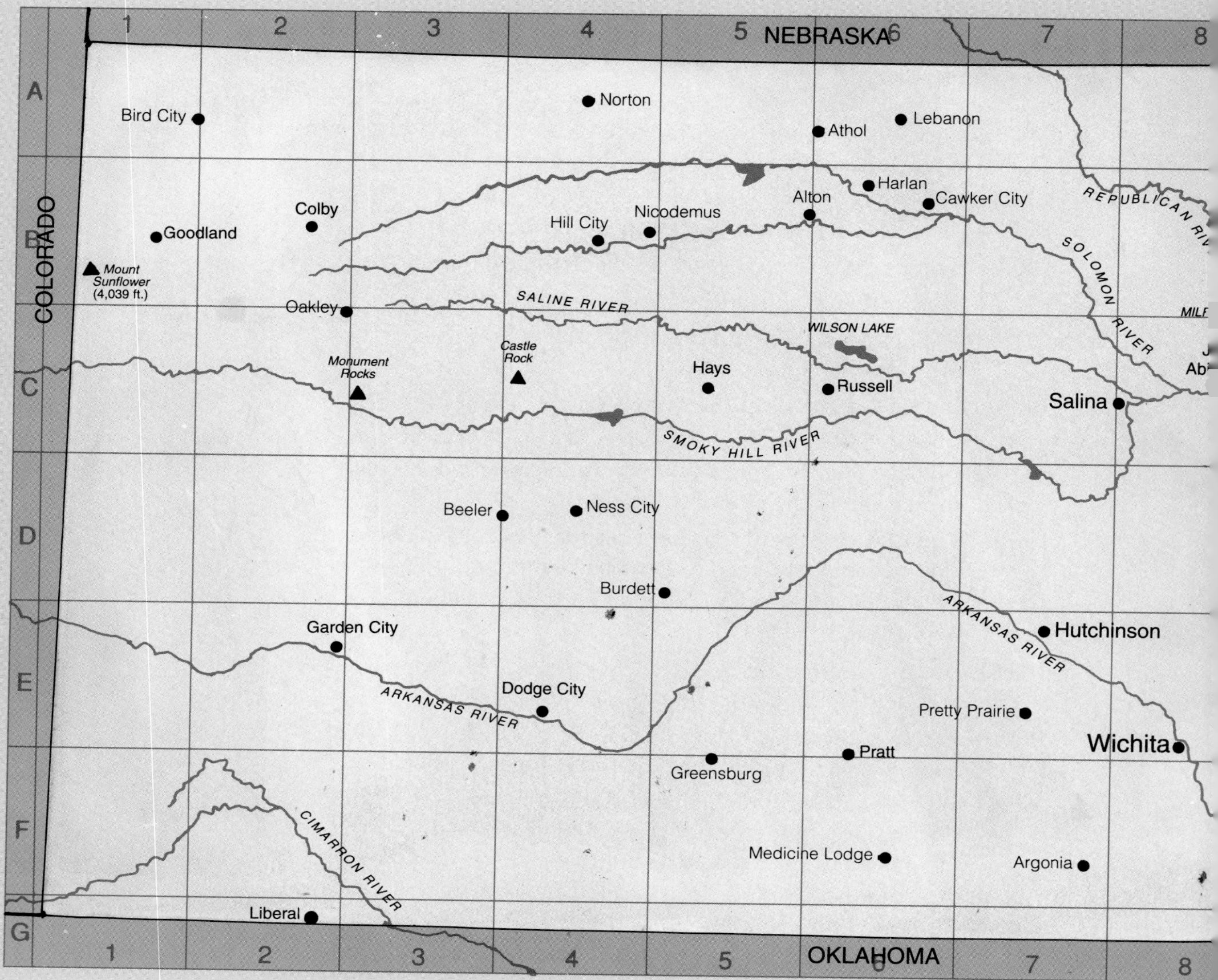

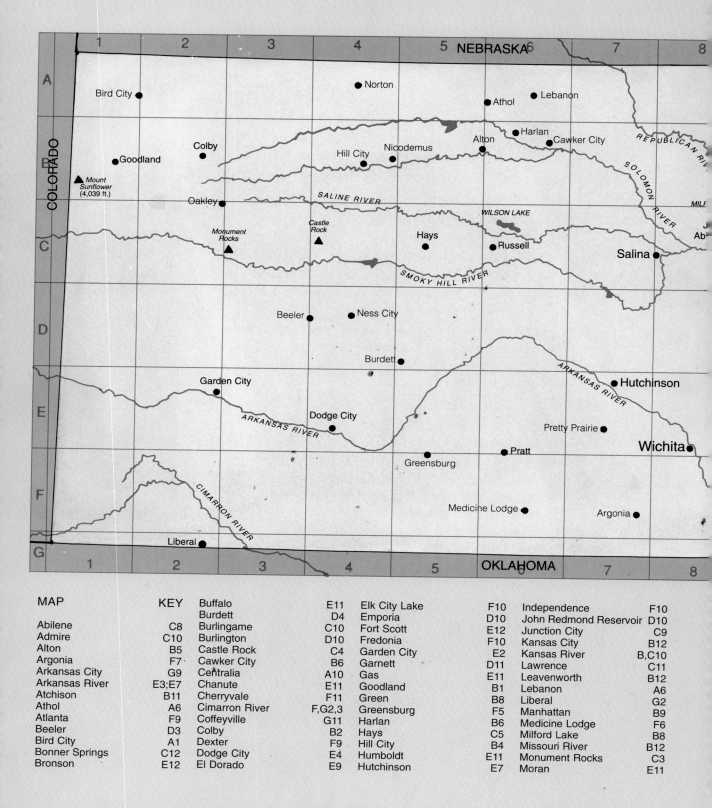

MAP KEY

Abilene	C8
Admire	C10
Alton	B5
Argonia	F7
Arkansas City	G9
Arkansas River	E3;E7
Atchison	B11
Athol	A6
Atlanta	F9
Beeler	D3
Bird City	A1
Bonner Springs	C12
Bronson	E12
Buffalo	E11
Burdett	D4
Burlingame	C10
Burlington	D10
Castle Rock	C4
Cawker City	B6
Centralia	A10
Chanute	E11
Cherryvale	F11
Cimarron River	F,G2,3
Coffeyville	G11
Colby	B2
Dexter	F9
Dodge City	E4
El Dorado	E9
Elk City Lake	F10
Emporia	D10
Fort Scott	E12
Fredonia	F10
Garden City	E2
Garnett	D11
Gas	E11
Goodland	B1
Green	B8
Greensburg	F5
Harlan	B6
Hays	C5
Hill City	B4
Humboldt	E11
Hutchinson	E7
Independence	F10
John Redmond Reservoir	D10
Junction City	C9
Kansas City	B12
Kansas River	B,C10
Lawrence	C11
Leavenworth	B12
Lebanon	A6
Liberal	G2
Manhattan	B9
Medicine Lodge	F6
Milford Lake	B8
Missouri River	B12
Monument Rocks	C3
Moran	E11

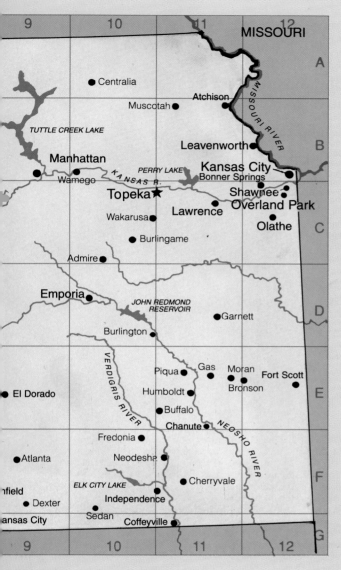

GLOSSARY

agriculture: Farming

antislavery: Against slavery

aquifer: An underground source of water

billion: A thousand million (1,000,000,000)

blizzard: A snowstorm driven by very high winds

capital: The city that is the seat of government

capitol: The building in which the government meets

climate: The typical weather of a region

conservation: The saving of natural resources

depression: A period of very hard times with widespread joblessness

drought: A period when rainfall is well below normal in an area

earth lodge: A grass-covered log house built by American Indians

glacier: A mass of slowly moving ice

hailstorm: A storm that drops ice lumps called hailstones or hail

integration: The process of bringing people of various races together

meteorite: Stone or metal that falls from space, striking the ground

million: A thousand thousand (1,000,000)

mural: A painting done directly on a wall

permanent: Lasting

pioneer: A person who is among the first to move into a region

plains: Rather flat lands

pollution: The harming or dirtying of natural resources

population: The number of people in a place

prairie: A grassland

proslavery: In favor of slavery

segregation: The process of keeping the races apart

slavery: A practice in which some people own other people

sod house: A home built from chunks of the ground

PICTURE ACKNOWLEDGMENTS

Front cover, ©**Tom Dietrich**; 1, ©David Muench/**Tony Stone Images, Inc.**; 2, **Tom Dunnington**; 3, ©Arni Katz/**Unicorn Stock Photos**; 4-5, **Tom Dunnington**; 6-7, ©**Tom Till**; 8, ©**Steve Mulligan**; 9 (left), ©Jim Shippee/**Unicorn Stock Photos**; 9 (right), **Courtesy of Hammond, Incorporated, Maplewood, New Jersey**; 10 (top), ©Barbara von Hoffmann/**Tom Stack & Associates**; 10 (bottom), ©**Steve Mulligan**; 11 (both pictures), ©**Steve Mulligan**; 12, **North Wind Picture Archives**, hand-colored; 13, ©**Steve Mulligan**; 14, **Photo courtesy of Business Men's Assurance Company of America, Kansas City, Missouri**; 15 (both pictures), ©**North Wind Pictures**, hand-colored halftones of the paintings by Peale; 16, ©**Tom Dietrich**; 17, 18 (both pictures), 19, 20, **Kansas State Historical Society**; 21 (top), **Stock Montage, Inc.**; 21 (bottom), 23, **Kansas State Historical Society**; 25, ©**Tom Dietrich**; 26, ©Eric R. Berndt/**N E Stock Photo**; 27, ©**Ron Welch**; 28 (top), ©Karl Kummels/**SuperStock**; 28 (bottom), ©**Cameramann International, Ltd.**; 29, ©**Tom Dietrich**; 30-31, ©**Steve Mulligan**; 33, ©Aneal Vohra/**Unicorn Stock Photos**; 34 (top), ©**Cameramann International, Ltd.**; 34 (bottom), ©Michael Massey/**Unicorn Stock Photos**; 35, ©James Blank/**Tony Stone Images, Inc.**; 36 (left), ©**Tom Dietrich**; 36 (right), ©David Fitzgerald/**Tony Stone Images, Inc.**; 37, ©**Ron Welch**; 38 (left), ©**Del Ruff**; 38 (right), ©Arni Katz/**Unicorn Stock Photos**; 39, ©Aneal Vohra/**Unicorn Stock Photos**; 40, ©James Blank/**Root Resources**; 42, ©Aneal Vohra/**Unicorn Stock Photos**; 43 (both pictures), ©**Steve Mulligan**; 44, **White House Historical Association/Photograph by the National Geographic Society**; 45, UPI/Bettmann; 46 (top), UPI/Bettmann Archive; 46 (bottom), AP/Wide World Photos; 47, **Stock Montage, Inc.**; 48 (both pictures), AP/**Wide World Photos**; 49 (both pictures), AP/**Wide World Photos**; 50 (top), UPI/Bettmann; 50 (bottom), AP/**Wide World Photos**; 51, AP/**Wide World Photos**; 52 (top), Bettmann; 52 (bottom), Reuters/Bettmann; 53, UPI/Bettmann; 54 (top), **Kansas Dept. of Revenue, Vehicle Division**; 54 (bottom), **Art provided by and reproduced with permission of Binney & Smith, maker of Crayola products**; 55, AP/**Wide World Photos**; 56 (top), **Courtesy Flag Research Center, Winchester, Massachusetts 01890**; 56 (middle), ©F.J. Baker/**Dembinsky Photo Assoc.**; 56 (bottom), ©Alan G. Nelson/**Root Resources**; 57 (top), ©Mark E. Gibson/**mga/Photri**; 57 (middle), ©**James P. Rowan**; 57 (bottom), ©Jeff Foott/**Tom Stack & Associates**; 58, **Kansas State Historical Society**; 59, AP/**Wide World Photos**; 60-61, **Tom Dunnington**; back cover, ©**Steve Mulligan**

INDEX

Page numbers in boldface type indicate illustrations.

ABOUT THE AUTHORS

Dennis and Judith Fradin have coauthored several books in the From Sea to Shining Sea series. The Fradins both graduated from Northwestern University in 1967. Dennis has been a professional writer for twenty years, and has published 150 books. His works for Childrens Press include the Young People's Stories of Our States series, the Disaster! series, and the Thirteen Colonies series. Judith earned her M.A. in literature from Northwestern University and taught high-school and college English for many years. The Fradins, who are the parents of Anthony, Diana, and Michael, live in Evanston, Illinois.

DATE DUE

45

13803

978.1   Fradin, Dennis B.
FRA

         Kansas

**LAKE ST SCHOOL MEDIA CENTER
VERNON, CONNECTICUT**